SIX-LEGGED NIGHTMARES

ASSASSIN BUGS KILL!

BY KRISTEN RAJCZAK NELSON

Gareth Stevens
PUBLISHING

Please visit our website, www.garethstevens.com. For a free color catalog of all our high-quality books, call toll free 1-800-542-2595 or fax 1-877-542-2596.

Cataloging-in-Publication Data

Names: Rajczak Nelson, Kristen.
Title: Assassin bugs kill! / Kristen Rajczak Nelson.
Description: New York : Gareth Stevens Publishing, 2018. | Series: Insects: six-legged nightmares | Includes index.
Identifiers: ISBN 9781538212479 (pbk.) | ISBN 9781538212493 (library bound) | ISBN 9781538212486 (6 pack)
Subjects: LCSH: Assassin bugs–Juvenile literature. | Predatory animals–Juvenile literature.
Classification: LCC QL523.R4 N45 2018 | DDC 595–dc23

First Edition

Published in 2018 by
Gareth Stevens Publishing
111 East 14th Street, Suite 349
New York, NY 10003

Copyright © 2018 Gareth Stevens Publishing

Designer: Laura Bowen
Editor: Ryan Nagelhout/Kate Mikoley

Photo credits: Cover, p. 1 (assassin bug) Spedona/Wikimedia Commons; cover, pp. 1-24 (background) Fantom666/Shutterstock.com; cover, pp. 1-24 (black splatter) Miloje/Shutterstock.com; cover, pp. 1-24 (web) Ramona Kaulitzki/Shutterstock.com; pp. 4-24 (text boxes) Tueris/Shutterstock.com; p. 5 Marco Uliana/Shutterstock.com; p. 7 (proboscis) Andr? De Kesel/Moment/Getty Images; p. 7 (wheel bug) Encyclopaedia Britannica/Universal Images Group/Getty Images; p. 9 (top) SIMON SHIM/Shutterstock.com; p. 9 (bottom) Meister Photos/Shutterstock.com; p. 11 Nathanael Siders/Shutterstock.com; p. 13 Katarina Christenson/Shutterstock.com; p. 15 David Maitland/Oxford Scientific/Getty Images; p. 17 (top) Jim H Walling/Shutterstock.com; p. 17 (bottom) Alex Sun/Shutterstock.com; p. 19 (top) rtsimage/Shutterstock.com; p. 19 (bottom) Sari ONeal/Shutterstock.com; p. 21 John Cancalosi/National Geographic Magazines/Getty Images.

Printed in China

CPSIA compliance information: Batch #CW18GS: For further information contact Gareth Stevens, New York, New York at 1-800-542-2595.

CONTENTS

Words in the glossary appear in **bold** type the first time they are used in the text.

AN ASSASSIN STRIKES!

As the assassin bug **stalks** its **prey**, it moves very carefully. It tries not to walk too regularly, so its steps might be mistaken for the wind blowing through the leaves. Then, it strikes! The prey never had a chance.

Assassin bugs are **insects** in the animal family Reduviidae (reh-juh-VY-uh-dee). There are thousands of species, or kinds, of bugs in this group, and many hunt their prey and kill it using a sharp beak that leaves the prey **paralyzed** and unable to fight their assassin!

TERRIFYING TRUTHS

An assassin is someone or something that kills with a sudden attack.

The many kinds of assassin bugs range in size from about 0.2 to 1.6 inches (0.5 to 4 cm).

BUG PARTS

Like all insects, assassin bugs have six legs. They have three body parts: a head, a middle part called the thorax, and an abdomen where the stomach is. They also have wings. You can spot an assassin bug because its head is connected to its thorax by a thin shape almost like a neck.

But the deadly part of the assassin bug is the long, needlelike beak, called a rostrum or proboscis. It's found between the bug's two front legs and is made up of three **segments**.

TERRIFYING TRUTHS

Assassin bugs may use their rostrum if they feel they're in danger, too.

Most assassin bugs, including wheel bugs like this one, are brown, black, or reddish. There are some that are more brightly colored, too!

antennae

head

proboscis

wings

legs

abdomen

thorax

wheel bug

LIFE OF THE ASSASSIN BUG

Assassin bugs have three parts to their life cycle: egg, nymph, and adult.

During the spring and early summer, assassin bugs leave their nests in the forest to find **mates**. Then, female assassin bugs lay bunches of eggs in the soil or on leaves. Nymphs, or young insects, come out of the eggs. They look like small, wingless adults.

Assassin bug nymphs **molt** between four and seven times and begin growing wings. They get bigger with each molt, soon becoming an adult.

TERRIFYING TRUTHS

Assassin bugs are found all over the world, including in North America.

assassin bug laying eggs

These assassin bug nymphs, shown below, will look much different after they molt several times!

assassin bug nymphs

9

ASSASSIN IN ACTION

Assassin bugs are sneaky hunters that look for food in trees, plants, and bushes. An assassin bug uses long body parts called antennae to find out more about what and where prey might be. Then, it moves carefully so the prey doesn't see or hear it. It grabs the prey with its front legs and sticks its sharp beak into the prey's body!

The assassin bug **injects** poison, or venom, into the prey through its rostrum. The venom takes affect in as few as 3 seconds!

TERRIFYING TRUTHS

Birds and large bugs, such as spiders and praying mantises, like to eat assassin bugs. Even other assassin bugs might snack on assassin bug nymphs!

If prey is this close to an assassin bug, it's likely too late already!

WHAT'S FOR LUNCH?

An assassin bug's prey may be completely paralyzed in as few as 15 seconds. It's still alive—but not for long! The assassin bug injects other matter to begin **digesting** the inside of the prey. It uses its rostrum like a straw to suck out the now-liquid insides! Yum!

Many species of assassin bugs like to eat other insects such as caterpillars, aphids, and beetles. However, some assassin bugs feed on the blood of **mammals**—including people!

TERRIFYING TRUTHS

Assassin bugs will eat just about any bug they can catch—unless they prefer mammals. Then, they may stick their rostrum into a bat for a snack!

Assassin bugs prey on small insects, as well as insects that might be larger than they are!

SPIDER KILLER

Giraffe assassin bugs are clever predators. They prey on another bug predator that's known to be tough to catch—spiders! Many spiders use webs to catch prey. They sense **vibrations** when the prey lands. But giraffe assassin bugs can approach the spider without it knowing!

The giraffe assassin bug first breaks one thread of a web. It keeps the ends of the thread tight to stop any vibrations. It slowly breaks more threads in this way until the spider is close enough to grab and stab!

TERRIFYING TRUTHS

Giraffe assassin bugs often break web threads when the wind is blowing so if there is any vibration from what they've done, the spider still won't notice!

Bee assassins hang out near flowers in order to get close to their favorite prey: bees!

SIT AND WAIT

Not all kinds of assassin bugs actively hunt! Ambush bugs lie in wait for their prey. They stay on flowers without moving until bees, flies, and other tasty bugs come near enough. Then, they use their front legs to grab their meal!

Some scientists put ambush bugs in their own group within Reduviidae. This is partly because ambush bugs are shorter and fatter than other assassin bugs. Ambush bugs' front legs are also thicker and look somewhat like a praying mantis's legs.

TERRIFYING TRUTHS

Since the 1980s, Ambush Bug has been the name of a comic book character who met superheroes such as Harley Quinn and Superman in his adventures.

Ambush bugs are often bright colors in order to blend in with flowers.

praying mantis

WHEEL BUGS

One of the biggest and most easily recognized assassin bugs is the wheel bug. It can grow to be 1.5 inches (3.8 cm) long and has a **crest** on its thorax that looks like a part inside a clock. Wheel bug nymphs have orange and black markings on their body, while adults are grey.

It's a good thing people can recognize wheel bugs—they bite! And their bite hurts a lot right away. If you ever see a wheel bug, don't try to pick it up.

TERRIFYING TRUTHS

Wheel bugs are quite common in the eastern United States.

Wheel bugs attack bigger bugs, including grasshoppers and large caterpillars.

AN UNWANTED KISS

Kissing bugs are likely the best-known assassin bug. They're also the most dangerous to us! Some kinds of kissing bugs carry Chagas disease, an illness that's caused by a **parasite**. They're mostly found in Central and South America.

Kissing bugs get their name because they tend to bite around people's faces, especially as they sleep. Some can become carriers of Chagas disease from drinking the blood of a person or animal with the illness. They pass it on through their waste.

TERRIFYING TRUTHS

Chagas disease can be deadly. But people can have it and not even show signs of it, too!

Kissing bugs hide in houses and come out at night!

GLOSSARY

crest: a showy growth on the head of an animal

digest: to break down food so the body can use it

inject: to force in

insect: a small, often winged, animal with six legs and three main body parts

mammal: a warm-blooded animal that has a backbone and hair, breathes air, and feeds milk to its young

mate: one of two animals that come together to produce babies

molt: the act of leaving behind a hard outer covering of an animal that has become too small

paralyzed: unable to move

parasite: a living thing that lives in, on, or with another living thing and often harms it

prey: an animal that is hunted by other animals for food. Also, to capture and eat prey.

segment: one part often joined to other parts like it

stalk: to walk carefully after something else

vibration: a rapid movement back and forth

FOR MORE INFORMATION

BOOKS

Klepeis, Alicia. *Assassin Bug vs. Orge-Faced Spider: When Cunning Hunters Collide*. North Mankato, MN: Capstone Press, 2016.

Rake, Matthew. *Creepy, Crawly Creatures*. Minneapolis, MN: Hungry Tomato, 2016.

WEBSITES

Insects
kids.nationalgeographic.com/animals/hubs/insects/
Find many different kinds of insects here.

White-Spotted Assassin Bug
kids.sandiegozoo.org/animals/insects/white-spotted-assassin-bug
Learn more about this interesting insect!

INDEX